REVISED AND UPDATED

Art In History

Ancient
Roman Art

Susie Hodge

Heinemann Library
Chicago, Illinois

Customer Service 888-454-2279
Visit our website at www.heinemannraintree.com

Design by Victoria Bevan, Michelle Lisseter, and Q2A Media
Illustrations by Oxford Illustrators
Printed and bound in Hong Kong by WKT

10 09 08 07 06
10 9 8 7 6 5 4 3 2 1

New edition ISBNs: 1 40348 767 7 (hardback)
                     1 40348 775 8 (paperback)

The Library of Congress has cataloged the first edition as follows:
Hodge, Susie, 1960–
        Ancient Roman art / Susie Hodge.
                p.   cm. -- (Art in history)
        Includes bibliographical references and index.
        Summary: Examines the art of ancient Rome, including painting,
mosaic, sculpture, and architecture.
        ISBN 1-57572-552-5 (lib. bdg.)
        I. Art. Roman--Juvenile literature. [I. Art, Roman. 2. Art,
Ancient.] I. Title. II. Series: Hodge, Susie, 1960–   Art in history.
N5760.H63   1997
709'.37--dc21   97–20673
                                                     CIP
                                                     AC

Acknowledgments
The publishers would like to thank the following for permission to reproduce photographs:
AKG photo, E. Lessing pp. **11** (right), **13**, **28**, Vatican Museums p. **4**; Art Arhive/Dagli Orti p. **11**; Ancient Art & Architecture Collection Ltd, R. Sheridan p. **10** (left); The Bridgeman Art Library, pp. **14–15**, Giraudon p. **19**, Metropolitan Museum of Art, New York p. **7**, Museo Archaeologico Nazionale, Naples pp. **6**, **11** (left), Museo & Gallerie Nazionali di Capodimonte, Naples p. **10** (right), Museum of Antiquities, Newcastle upon Tyne p. **9**; Corbis, R. Ergenbright p. **25**, R. Nowitz p. **27**, R. Vanni p. **26**, A. Woolfitt p. **20**; C. M. Dixon pp. **18**, **24**; Giraudon pp. **22–23**, Lauros pp. **5**, **12**, **21**, Mermet p. **8**; Michael Holford p. **29**; Photo Scala p. **17**.

Cover picture of Hera, Thena, and Aphrodite, mosaic reproduced with permission of The Art Archive/Musee du Louvre, Paris/Dagli Orti.

Every effort has been made to contact copyright holders of any material reproduced in this book. Any omissions will be rectified in subsequent printings if notice is given to the publishers.

The paper used to print this book comes from sustainable resources.

CONTENTS

Some words are shown in bold, **like this**.
You can find out what they mean by looking in the glossary.

WHAT IS ROMAN ART?

Near the Tiber River in Italy, several small villages on seven hills grew to become the city of Rome. By 509 BC Rome was a **republic**. Gradually, its power grew until it became a vast **empire**. By AD 100, Rome ruled over most of the then known world.

Adopting traditions

The Romans took over many countries, including Carthage (in North Africa), Gaul (which stretched from Italy to the Netherlands), Greece, Egypt, and Britain. They adopted the traditions in these countries that appealed to them, such as the religion or art. Romans ruled, organized, and taxed the people of these countries, often mixing the best of Rome with the best of other cultures.

Many people from Rome's captive countries were employed by the Romans. Greek and Egyptian artists, for example, used their own methods to produce art for the Romans.

This statue of the first Roman emperor Augustus (31 BC – AD 14) was made by a Greek sculptor. The Romans admired the dignity of Greek **portraits** in statue form. They wanted their emperor shown as a commanding, godlike person. The back of this statue was unfinished, because Roman statues stood against walls.

Augustus, Prima Porta near Rome, c. 19 BC, 6 feet, 8 inches (2.04 m), **marble**

Lifelike details

The Romans took on other traditions, but added their own likes and dislikes. They admired the beauty and perfection of Greek art, but they preferred lifelike details that showed people's oddities and character.

The Triumphal Arch of Tiberius, southern France, c. AD 30, height 60 feet (18.3 m), stone

Arches to proclaim victories were set up all over the Roman Empire. These and other buildings were designed with different sized arches and columns to make them more interesting to look at.

Powerful achievements

The Romans employed artists and workmen throughout their empire to produce impressive art and to build great roads and buildings. Art and **architecture** were used to honor the gods, to celebrate events, or to proclaim someone's power. They were not just for decoration—although that was also important. It is a sign of Roman power that their style remained similar in different lands. The Romans have had an enormous influence on art and architecture.

MATERIALS AND METHODS

Who became an artist?

Architects (master builders and designers) were usually educated people of the middle class. They created some of the grandest monuments in the history of architecture. Other artists (all called craftsmen) were usually poorer **citizens**. They worked in small workshops with a few **apprentices** and one or two slaves. Many Greek artists set up workshops so that Roman artists could learn from them. Most paintings or statues were commissioned, or ordered, by wealthy citizens. Artists rarely signed their work, because they felt they were only doing a job. Artists were not thought to be special.

A **bust** is a statue of the head and shoulders. Roman artists made a portrait of anyone who could afford to pay them. They did not try to make portraits perfect, but rather enjoyed showing a person's characteristics. Even though he was the emperor, this bust shows Vespasian's wrinkled skin, large nose, and serious expression. Statues of emperors were put up all over the empire as a reminder that the Romans were in control.

Bust of Emperor Vespasian, c. AD 75, marble

Garden of Livia, Prima Porta near Rome,
c. 50–40 BC, height 5 feet (1.52 m), fresco

This is one of many wall paintings discovered in a
Roman house. It is filled with fruit trees, flowers, and
birds. Bluish colors help to show distance and space,
brighter colors seem close up, and shadows make some
objects look solid.

What materials did artists work with?

Brushes were made from twigs, wood, lengths of reeds (tall grasses),
or rushes (marsh plants). They were sometimes bound with hair.
Artists used shaped wood and ivory sticks for drawing and writing.
These were called styluses. Many wall paintings were made of paint
mixed with egg yolk, called tempera. Some were in encaustic, which
means that colors are mixed with wax and burned into the surface
with hot irons. But most were painted in **fresco**.

For tempera and encaustic, the walls had to be smooth. Artists
prepared them with a coating of cement, **plaster**, and marble dust,
which they polished before painting it. For frescoes, artists coated
walls with plaster. They then applied the paint while the plaster was
wet. Most statues were polished and then painted in tempera.

SIGNS AND SYMBOLS

Many of our words and alphabet letters come from Latin, which was the common language of the Roman Empire. Having one common language meant that people from different countries could communicate with one another.

Most Roman citizens were encouraged to learn to read. In large cities like Rome and Alexandria, there were many bookstores, libraries, and publishers.

Virgil and the Muses, AD *end of the 100s to the early 200s, mosaic*

This **mosaic** shows the famous poet Virgil sitting between two muses. Muses are goddesses who inspire writers and artists. Virgil holds a papyrus scroll of his greatest poem, The Aeneid.

How books were made

Books were usually **scrolls** made out of papyrus, an Egyptian marsh plant. The reed was cut into long, narrow strips, soaked and pressed together, beaten with a mallet, left to dry, and finally polished smooth with a stone.

Each book had to be written out by hand. Someone read the book to several scribes, who copied the book down. Each scribe made a copy on the papyrus using reed pens. The Latin words were written in columns. Some of the scribes were artists, too, and many books were beautifully illustrated.

Roman letters

Scribes (writers) and stonemasons painted or carved inscriptions (words) on their monuments and statues. They used two main kinds of letters: square capital letters for formal inscriptions, and sloping italic letters for informal writing, such as letter-writing. Each letter was made of a geometric shape, such as a square, triangle, or circle. At first, letters in stone were carved to one thickness. Later, the sides were made to vary from thick to thin. This gave the same effect as the square-tipped brushes that stonemasons used to paint the letters on the stone first.

Inscription from Milecastle, on Hadrian's Wall, Great Britain, AD *122–125, stone*

A castle was built every mile along Hadrian's Wall. This inscription records the building of one milecastle (small fort) by the Second Legion Augusta. The letters were chiseled by hand and the little tick-shaped marks at the ends of letters are where stonemasons rested their chisels as they carved. We use tick-shapes even now on some printed letters and call them serifs.

PAINTING TECHNIQUES

The Romans loved to have paintings in their homes and public buildings. They did not have wallpaper, so artists painted pictures directly onto the walls and ceilings. They also painted floors. People hung small panel paintings on wood on walls or displayed them on **easels**. These were sold from artists' workshops.

Fresco was used for most walls. This made the colors brighter and helped the painting to last. When the background was dry, artists added details. They painted all kinds of scenes, such as gods and heroes, hunting and farming, landscapes, and animals. Portraits of the owners of houses were also popular.

Trick pictures
Four different styles of Roman wall painting developed.

First style Artists painted walls to look as if they were made of marble or were copies of Greek styles of decoration.

Second style Realistic-looking scenes tricked the eye. They looked like views through windows.

House of Citharist, Stabiae, Naples, c. 100-0 BC, fresco

This house had a series of frescoes running around it that were similar to Greek homes. Some houses had marbled effects painted on the walls.

Room from the Villa of Mysteries, Pompeii, c. 50 BC, height 5 feet (1.5 m), fresco

The background of brilliant red and the black dividing lines do not look realistic, but the life-sized figures certainly do. Twenty-nine figures and many scenes run continuously around the room, making it appear larger than it really is.

Third style This included less realistic, but often delicate looking pictures.

Fourth style This was a combination of the second and third styles.

Spring, Maiden Gathering Flowers, Stabiae, Naples, c. 15 BC – AD 60, fresco

Roman Lady from the House of the Vettii, Pompeii, c. AD 0-79, fresco

This might be a goddess or simply the lady of the house picking flowers as if in a dance. Gracefully draped in a colored robe, she is painted in a gentle, fresh style.

This fresco shows a Roman lady. It was found on a wall in the remains of a house in Pompeii, along with many similiar frescoes.

Paint palette
Paints were made from ground rocks, powdered plants, or animal dyes. Red and yellow came from ocher (a clay-like substance), white came from chalk, green from green earth, blue from a mixture of glass and copper, black from soot, and purple from a special seashell. The **pigments** were mixed with lime, milk, egg, or gum to make a paste.

STORYTELLING PICTURES

In addition to inscriptions and books, the Romans used paintings and **reliefs** to tell stories of their war victories. The Greeks had also done this. But where the Greeks used **symbolism** to tell their stories, the Romans showed the real, sometimes gory, details.

Ancient customs

Narrative, or storytelling, pictures had been a custom hundreds of years before in China. During those times, kings ordered monuments announcing their victories in war. Later, these monuments developed into complete picture-stories. Wealthy Romans liked the idea of proclaiming Roman triumphs for all to see. Artists were employed to paint or carve heroic stories.

Trajan's Column, Rome, AD 113, height 125 feet (38 m), marble

Emperor Trajan ordered a huge column to be made to show the story of his wars. As in a comic strip, Trajan appears in a continuous, lively story that spirals around the column.

Artists from Africa made this large floor mosaic. The most important part of the picture is the figures. Their hair and clothes and the animals' fur and feathers are detailed, although the trees and rocks are small and decorative. Trying to make the picture look realistic was not the aim. The picture was meant to tell a story and look attractive.

Public and private art

Works of art that showed the Roman Empire and its emperors as strong and generous were put in public places for all to see. Storytelling pictures were painted inside private houses by interior decorators, not major artists.

Art for everyone

Like advertising today, these great works of art convinced and persuaded people. They proudly announced victories. At the same time, they told people that the Roman Empire was the greatest.

Most narrative art was about battles. Some stories of gods, goddesses, heroes, and legends were also painted and carved. Roman art was meant to be seen and enjoyed by many. Artists worked hard at making it easy to understood.

MOSAIC ART

Mosaics became popular from 0–100 AD. They were pictures or patterns made from small pieces of colored glass or stone. They decorated walls and floors.

How mosaics were made

Artists drew a design of the mosaic they were going to make. Then, they spread wet plaster over a small area of the floor or wall and smoothed it down. They quickly pressed the pieces of stone into the plaster while it was still damp, following their design.

At first, patterns in black and white were the most common. They remained fashionable around Rome. But by the 100s AD, more colorful mosaics became popular in areas farther away. Companies of artists designed mosaics in their workshops. People chose a design, then the mosaic artist came to the house with the chosen plan and the stones already cut. Several artists would work on one mosaic.

Orpheus Playing to the Animals, *Antioch in Turkey, c.* AD *100s, mosaic*

The Roman god Orpheus plays a lyre, charming the animals around him. Shadows and highlights make the picture look three-dimensional. See how contented all the animals look as they listen to the music!

Brightly colored pieces of stone called tesserae have turned this wall into a beautifully decorated area. It is meant to be more of a pattern than realistic, although you can clearly see what it represents. Mosaics in this style were used to decorate fountains, too.

Bird and Bunch of Grapes, Badajoz in Spain, c. 350 BC, mosaic

Make your own mosaic

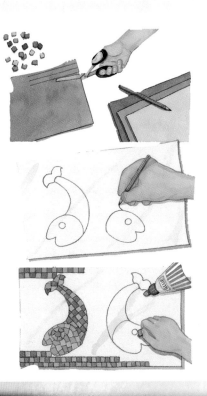

Materials:
- **Several sheets of colored paper or posterboard**
- **Scissors**
- **Glue**
- **Large sheets of white paper or posterboard**
- **Pencil**

1. Cut the colored paper or posterboard into small squares.
2. Draw your mosaic outline on a large sheet of white paper or posterboard.
3. Glue the colored squares in place on your outline, leaving a tiny space between each of your squares, so that the mosaic looks realistic.

ART FOR THE GODS

The Romans adopted religions as well as styles of art from the countries they took over. They gave their adopted gods and goddesses different names. For example, Aphrodite was the Greek goddess of love and beauty. The Romans called her Venus. Until Christianity was adopted, the Romans did not believe in worshiping just one god. Because of this, it made sense to allow the people in the country they took over to keep their own gods.

The Romans did not believe that their art showed real events. They were made to remind people about the gods they were worshiping and to please the gods themselves. Some pictures showed people performing rituals for the gods. Some showed wondrous stories of supernatural strength and power. Some, such as the figures on the breastplate of Augustus on page 4, showed that the gods protected the good and the great.

Mars and Venus, from the House of Lucrezio Frontone, Pompeii, AD *0–79, fresco*

According to Roman religion, Mars, the god of war, loved Venus. Roman artists often painted the two together, sometimes showing them as ordinary humans. In this image, Mars stands behind wearing military dress, with a helmet. Venus, sitting in front of him, wears a long tunic and light cloak, like a wealthy Roman woman. Cupid, the god of love, stands in the center, while other citizens look on.

Marriage of Zeus and Hera on Mount Ida, Naples, Museo Nazionale

Hera, queen of the gods, was Zeus's wife and the goddess of marriage. It was not a happy marriage between the two gods. Hera hated Zeus so much that she caused him problems at every opportunity.

Household gods

The Romans worshiped thousands of gods and spirits. The most important gods and goddesses were Jupiter, Neptune, Venus, and Minerva. They were well known to Roman citizens throughout the empire because all kinds of art had been made in the gods' honor. Apart from the main gods, every house had its own shrine, called a Lararium. At this shrine, the people worshiped the household gods, called Lares, every day. The Lararium was often carved and decorated with small statuettes and painted friezes (decorations that run in a band).

ROMAN SCULPTURE

Sculptors and stonemasons were hired to make statues for public buildings and private villas. Statues were brightly painted, but the paint has now worn off. Gods, goddesses, animals, and portraits of real people were common subjects.

Titus, Rome, c. AD 80, height 6 feet, 5 inches (1.96 m), marble

This portrait of Emperor Titus was part of a full-length sculpture. By looking stern and mighty, the image commanded everyone to look up to it. It was made to show his power and importance.

Roman Butcher, c. 200–100 BC, stone frieze

This relief probably decorated a Roman butcher's shop. The butcher is chopping meat on a block. You can see other types of meat hanging on hooks above. Notice the little details that the artist has included, such as the pulley and rope and the folds of the butcher's toga.

Scenes from everyday life

Roman artists also carved details from daily life. Often these were made for sarcophagi (stone coffins) or tombstones to tell stories of a dead person's life. These relief carvings show scenes like mothers bathing their babies, people working or relaxing, or wedding ceremonies. They all seem natural looking and relaxed. They also give us a wonderful insight into everyday Roman life.

Commemorative statues

There was great demand for **commemorative** statues. They were placed in public squares, halls, or temples. Some were put on top of commemorative columns. Most were of emperors and other important people, and they symbolized victory and power. Sculptors had learned from Greek sculptors how to show draped material over what appears to be a living body. They enjoyed the challenge of creating realistic-looking fabric hanging in folds on the body, as well as creating realistic-looking faces. Along with statues in armor, these portrait statues were grand and lifelike reminders of the rulers of the Roman Empire.

CLASSICAL STYLE

The term *classical art* usually refers to the art of the ancient Greeks and Romans. The classical style is carefully designed and balanced.

Borrowing ideas

The Romans copied the Greeks, but the Greeks originally learned from the Egyptians. They borrowed Egyptian ideas, but were able to improve such crafts as marble carving and **bronze casting** because they had better tools. This allowed them to create more realistic images than the Egyptians. The Romans then borrowed and adapted the Greeks' ideas.

Marcus Aurelius, AD *161–80, height 11 ft., 6 in. (3.5 m), bronze*

This is the only large-scale Roman bronze statue that has survived to the present day. After the Romans converted to Christianity, bronze statues of non-Christian emperors or gods were melted down. This statue was mistakenly believed to be of a Christian emperor, so it was not destroyed. Notice the emperor's striking pose and the lifelike horse. The whole weight of the rider and horse is carried on three thin legs. This was a difficult effect to produce.

Detailed descriptions

A scribe named Pliny, who lived from about AD 23 to 79, wrote an encyclopedia of natural sciences and arts. He described many Roman artists and their methods, such as the casting of bronze. Pliny's book was useful to artists centuries later. They learned skills that might otherwise have been forgotten.

The Romans loved art and color. Most statues were brightly painted originally, but the color has now worn away. Sculptors produced many beautifully draped female forms like the one to the right. They concentrated on proportion and balance and made every feature stand out clearly.

The goddess Hecate, Yugoslavia, c. AD 0-100, marble

Skilled sculptors

Sculptors became highly skilled, drawing many sketches, then making clay, wax, or plaster maquettes (small test models of the sculpture). They used marble, bronze, wood, and wax for most statues and reliefs. Sculptors often used the lost-wax method of casting. First, sculptors made a model in wax. Then, they made a clay mold around it. When baked, the wax melted away and the clay became the mold for the bronze to be poured into. The artist later broke open the clay mold to reveal the solid bronze statue.

SCULPTURE FOR ALL

At first it was customary to carry wax images of ancestors (relatives) in Roman funeral processions. Romans believed that this preserved the dead person's soul. Later, when the empire stretched to distant lands, Romans burned incense in front of busts of their emperors, treating them like gods. Sacrifices were also brought to shrines for their gods. This proved the people's faith and devotion.

Claudius, AD 51–54, life-size, marble

When new, this sculpture would have been full-length, brightly painted, and polished. Roman sculptors produced lifelike statues of their emperors. Many later emperors thought of themselves as gods. They told their people that they should be worshiped as gods. Whether or not people really believed they were gods, it was safer to act as if they did!

Statues everywhere

Romans put sculpture on display everywhere. Many sculptures were portraits. Others, like Trajan's Column on page 12, were reliefs that told a story, often one of Roman triumph. All these sculptures were a form of reporting and **propaganda**. They reminded people of the power of the Roman Empire.

Most sculptures were more than just decoration. Sea creatures, such as dolphins, which symbolized the god Cupid, were built into fountains. Gods, goddesses, heroes, and animals appeared in town squares (called forums), temples, public buildings, and houses. Often forums displayed statues of the town's patron god.

Detail from The Ara Pacis Augustae, 19–13 BC, height 5 feet, 3 inches (1.6 m), marble relief

The Ara Pacis Augustae was a large marble altar given by Emperor Augustus. It was dedicated to peace and to the people. Patterns and reliefs of stories are carved in detail on the walls. The stories are a mix of truth and legend. It shows Augustus, his wife, children, grandchildren (who were future emperors), and the chief priest. Notice how the people in the background are carved faintly, while those in the foreground are clearer.

Families

The family was important to the Romans. Statues and paintings of family members, alive and dead, were made and displayed in their homes and gardens. Statues of the Lares, gods of the household, were also shown.

23

ROMAN BUILDINGS

Early Roman towns had no particular plan. But as the empire grew and became more organized, the Romans began to arrange their towns. They needed public baths, meeting places, government buildings, and temples for worship. A style for towns was developed. The most important public buildings were placed around a central forum (square). The rest of the town spread out from the forum in a grid pattern.

Columns and arches

The Romans used five types of column for important buildings. They were adapted from Greek columns. Roman architects and engineers also figured out how to build **domes**, **vaults**, and arches.

Arches span wider gaps and support more weight than the straight beams of wood or stone that had been used previously. So, with arches, Roman buildings grew larger and stronger.

The Baths of Caracalla, Rome, AD 212, originally stone, glass, concrete, and marble

There were public baths throughout the Roman Empire, but the ones in Rome were decorated particularly magnificently. It is hard to imagine now, but in Roman times, this ruin was a richly decorated and popular building (big enough for 1,600 people). There were hot, warm, and cold baths, as well as exercise and lecture rooms, libraries, and snack bars. You can still see the remains of the vaulted ceilings. Vaulted ceilings were arches overlapping at right angles.

This is another great achievement in Roman building. It is an aqueduct. It was 25 miles (40 km) long and built to channel water to the town of Nîmes in France. Three tiers of arches cross the Gard River. Many similar aqueducts were built throughout the empire to bring fresh water to towns.

The Pont du Gard, Agrippa, France, 19 BC, height 162 feet (49.4 m), stone

A strong invention

The Greeks had used stone for building, but the Romans developed concrete. They made it with lime, sand, and water, plus small stones, pieces of rock, or pottery. Because concrete could be spread smoothly before drying, architects were able to develop new curved shapes on wooden frames.

By 200–100 BC, Roman builders added powdered volcanic stone (called pumice) to make a concrete that was strong and waterproof. Architects coated the outside of concrete buildings with polished brick or marble.

BIG BUILDINGS

New building methods meant that Roman buildings and monuments were strong. Roman architects were the first to build high-rise apartment blocks!

The Pantheon, Rome, built in AD 125, replacing a smaller temple from 27 BC, concrete, brick, and marble

This new form of temple was originally planned by Emperor Augustus's lieutenant, Agrippa. It was eventually completed when Hadrian was emperor. It is a masterpiece of art and engineering. The domed ceiling is surprisingly large. It is 141 feet (43 m) across. It was meant to represent the curved canopy (roof) of heaven. In the center, a hole, 28 feet (8.5 m) across, provides light and air.

Tools and equipment

The Romans developed ways of mass producing bricks in standard sizes and shapes. They baked triangular-shaped bricks in **kilns** to make them last longer than ordinary sun-dried bricks. They baked tiles and gutters from clay in a similar way. They often used bricks set in cement in arches, domes, and vaults.

Various tools, such as the **groma**, were used to estimate straight lines. Wooden scaffolding was used to support builders as they worked to keep blocks of stone in place. The Romans even used wooden cranes to help lift and position heavy objects. The cranes were driven by treadmills and linked to pulleys.

Huge arena

One of the most famous Roman buildings is the huge arena in Rome known as the Colosseum. Arches, vaults, and concrete meant that architects could design and build this spectacular sight. It was covered in gleaming white marble, with statues in every arch.

The Colosseum was used for shows that featured gladiators or animals fighting, or the execution of enemies of the empire. During the intermission, spectators were sprinkled with perfume to mask the smell of blood from the arena.

The Colosseum, Rome, AD *72–80, height 159 feet (48.5 m), stone and concrete*

The Colosseum seated 50,000 spectators. Beneath the ground, a huge network of chambers housed the animals and people before their performances. The arena could even be flooded for mock naval battles. The foundations were 39 feet (12 m) deep. Columns were added all around the **auditorium**. Research suggests that there could have been a movable canopy that covered the open area to shade it from the sun.

EARLY CHRISTIAN ART

Christians, unlike most other religious groups, worshiped only one god. This meant that they refused to worship the emperor. So, at first the Romans tried to stamp out Christianity. But the number of Christians grew. In AD 312 the new emperor, Constantine, became a Christian himself and made Christianity legal. Art began to change.

The Miracle of the Loaves and Fishes, *Ravenna, Italy, c. AD 520, mosaic*

When Christianity was accepted, artists began using Bible stories as subjects. This shows the New Testament story of when Jesus fed 5,000 people with five loaves of bread and two fish. The Romans tried to make Christianity acceptable by using familiar images from other religions. Jesus, in this picture, is copied from the old Roman god Apollo.

Secret art
For many years, Christians had to worship in secret. They met in catacombs (underground passageways). They designed secret symbols and included them in paintings of Bible stories on the walls of the catacombs.

Symbol of Christianity, Lullingstone Villa, Kent, England, late AD 300s, wall painting, fresco

A strange mixture

We know that Roman artists could make true-to-life images, but the picture on the opposite page looks stiff. There are shadows on the ground and in the folds of cloth, but other lifelike details were apparently no longer considered necessary. Artists felt it was more important to use recognizable symbols than to produce realistic art.

Church design

Christians modeled their churches on basilicas (large, rectangular assembly halls). These became the basic design for Christian churches everywhere. Statues in new churches were discouraged. However, because many people could not read or write, paintings and reliefs taught them about their new religion.

The end of classical art

It was not just Roman art that was changing. The empire had grown too big and its emperors could not control it. The Roman army began to retreat from the countries around the edges of the empire. Gradually, the empire crumbled and other people took over, bringing new ideas with them.

TIMELINE

BC

753	Legendary date of when Rome was founded.
509	Last king is forced out of Rome; a republic is formed.
500	Romans begin to take over neighboring parts of Italy.
265	Rome controls the whole of Italy.
204	Rome invades Africa.
202	Rome seizes parts of Spain.
179	First stone bridge over the Tiber River.
140	Romans conquer Greece and most of Spain.
59–51	Gaul is conquered.
55	Britain is invaded.
50–40	*Garden of Livia* is painted. Wall paintings in the Villa of Mysteries, Pompeii, are made.
30	Conquest of Egypt takes place.
27	Augustus becomes the first emperor (beginning of the Roman Empire).
25	Agrippa, Augustus's lieutenant and son-in-law, designs a temple in Rome.
19	The Pont du Gard aqueduct is designed and built by Agrippa.
13–9	The Ara Pacis Augustae altar is built (commissioned by Emperor Augustus).
5	Jesus is born in Bethlehem.

AD

14	Tiberius becomes emperor.
30	The Triumphal Arch of Tiberius is built. Many monuments, reliefs, and inscriptions are produced to tell stories of victories.
41–54	Britain is conquered. Busts and portraits of the emperors are worshipped as gods.
54–68	Emperor Nero rules and tries to get rid of all Christians.
72–80	The Colosseum is designed and built.
79–81	Titus is emperor. The volcano Vesuvius erupts (AD 79), destroying the towns of Herculaneum and Pompeii on the west coast of Italy.
101	Trajan becomes emperor and commissions his column.
117–138	Hadrian is emperor. He builds a wall separating Britain and Scotland. The Pantheon is built on the site of Agrippa's earlier temple in Rome.
138–312	Many emperors rule. Plague, famine, and wars interrupt peace and power.
312–37	Emperor Constantine rules. He becomes Christian and stops the persecution of Christians. Christian art is no longer secret art.
337–64	Many other emperors rule.
410	Roman Empire is reduced. Unrest continues.

GLOSSARY

apprentice person learning a trade or craft by working with a skilled worker

architecture art of designing and constructing buildings

auditorium part of a theater where the audience (the people watching) sit or stand

bronze long-lasting brownish gold metal. It is a mixture of copper and tin.

bust sculpture of just the head and shoulders of a person

casting producing a sculpture from a mold

citizen inhabitant of a city who had many legal, political, and other privileges. Not everyone was classed as a citizen. Slaves, for example, were non-citizens and had no privileges.

commemorative way of keeping things in people's memories. Memorials and celebrations are commemorative.

dome vault rising up from a round base, usually shaped like one half of a hollow ball

easel stand or support for holding paintings

empire land ruled by an emperor

fresco painting made on damp, freshly plastered walls

groma surveying tool used for measuring the land

kiln extremely hot oven used to bake or fire clay to harden it

marble hard rock that can be polished to a high shine. It comes in many patterns and colors.

mosaic picture or design made by cementing together small pieces of glass, ceramics, or stone of different colors. It was used on floors and walls.

pigment colored powder made from plants, minerals, or animals and mixed with various liquids to make paint

plaster fine white powder made from a rock called gypsum. It is mixed with water, then left to dry.

portrait picture or sculpture of a particular person or people

propaganda publicity that spreads ideas or information that will influence people

relief raised, carved pictures

republic country without a hereditory ruler

scroll book written on a long sheet of paper (or papyrus) that is rolled up

symbolism pictures using symbols for meanings, rather than real, factual images

vault curved ceiling made by arches. A barrel or tunnel vault is a group of arches together. A groin vault is two barrel vaults crossing at right angles.

FIND OUT MORE

You can find out more about Roman art in books and on the Internet. Use a search engine such as www.yahooligans.com to search for information. A search for the words "ancient Roman art" will bring back lots of results, but it may be difficult to find the information you want. Try refining your search to look for some of the ideas mentioned in this book, such as "frescoes."

More books to read

Chrisp, Peter. *Ancient Rome*. Chicago: Raintree, 2005

Macdonald, Fiona. *Ancient Rome*. Chicago: Heinemann Library, 2005

INDEX

Numbers in plain type (24) refer to the text.

Numbers in bold type (**28**) refer to an illustration.